My Moments with God

MERLINE RAPLEY

ISBN 978-1-955156-11-0 (paperback)
ISBN 978-1-955156-12-7 (hardcover)
ISBN 978-1-955156-13-4 (digital)

Copyright © 2021 by Merline Rapley

All rights reserved. No part of this publication may be reproduced, distributed, or transmitted in any form or by any means, including photocopying, recording, or other electronic or mechanical methods without the prior written permission of the publisher. For permission requests, solicit the publisher via the address below.

Rushmore Press LLC
1 800 460 9188
www.rushmorepress.com

Printed in the United States of America

Dedication

I dedicate this book to the Almighty God, and I hope that I have made Him proud; all of my thoughts came from Him. To my children: DeEvra P. Knight Wilson; to whom I owe so much for her hard work and encouragement, to my son Keith D. Knight, my grandchildren: Richarre M. Mayo, Richard L. Mayo II, and Anton Knight, and great grandson Trayson.

My prayer is that you will all stay with God. Hold on to His unchanging hand; He is real and His word is true. If you ever need Him, and you will, there is nothing that He can't do. Trust Him.

Love and Prayers Always, Mom, Grandmother
and Great Grandmother

Today He is nearer, and so much dearer
In my heart He is sweeter than ever before

"God spoke to me audibly, and said,
"I want my people back."

Table of Contents

Our Creator 1
Creation 2
The End-The Beginning 3
God Was, Is, and Always Will be. 4
Women of God: Distortion and Fulfillment 5
Ruth 1:16 (KJV) 6
Have Faith in God 7
David 8
Solomon 9
Thoughts About God 10
Behold the Lamb. 11
Don't Judge 12
Luke 1:30-31 (KJV) 13
Psalm 119:92 (KJV) 14
Abomination. 15
The Battle Is The Lord's 16
Who Is To Blame? 17
Haggai 1:11 (KJV) 18
Be Humble and Upright 19
Psalm 25:20-21 (KJV). 20
Deliverance 21
God Cares. 22
Lord Help Us To Stand 23
Chosen People. 24
Comfort 25
This Life 26
Satan. 27
A Follower of Christ 28
Use What God Gives You 29

Lift Up Jesus	30
Obey	31
Run On	32
Changed	33
Revelation 22:3 (KJV)	34
Psalm 46:10 (KJV)	35
Romans 6:11 (KJV)	36
Romans 12:1 (KJV)	37
Deuteronomy 5:32 (NKJV)	38
Warranty	39
Do Not Be Afraid	40
I Am	41
Spiritual Thoughts	42
Here Am I Lord	43
Baby Jesus	44
Numbers 14:9 (KJV)	45
Numbers 14:24 (KJV)	46
Our Journey	47
Psalm 150:6 (KJV)	48
Philippians 2:3 (KJV)	49
Not Your Glory	50
The Power of Love	51
Lord Save Us!	52
Beauty in The Desert	53
Wrinkles	54
Thanksgiving and Praise	55
If God Is Not In You, He Is Not In The Building	56
Haggai 1:13 (KJV)	57
One Prayer at A Time	58
In Your Own Time	59
God's Grace	60
Faith	61

Steppin High	62
I Never Got the Church in Me	63
My Intercessor	64
Spiritual Thoughts	65
God Is Using You	66
Light in the Lord	67
Be Prepared	68
Stay in The Race	69
First Encounter	70
Pressing On	71
God's Candles	72
He Lives	73
Three in One	74
Doubt	75
We Can't Hide	76
Psalm 139:14(KJV)	77
A Holy Life	78
Submission	79
In God's Service	80
Just A Thought	81
Philippians 3:18-19 (KJV)	82
Mark 9:20 (KJV)	83
Press Toward the Mark	84
If	85
Lord We Need You So	86
Psalm 119:2 (KJV)	87
Vain Glory	88
God's Love	89
A Friend	90
It's Over	91
Forgiveness	92
Blackness	93

God Wants Us All To Be Winners	94
Disciples	95
Matthew 8:5-6 (KJV)	96
Psalm 119:23 (KJV)	97
I'm Up High, Now I Can Breathe	98
I Corinthians 13:1-3 (KJV)	99
Bigots	100
Peace In The Midst of A Storm	101
I Am Your Vessel	102
Psalm 119:92-93 (KJV)	103
Spiritual Thoughts	104
He Will Never Leave Us or Forsake Us	105
Hear and Obey	106
Be A Faithful Witness	107
Sin	108
Power	109
The Whole Armour of God	110
Stand	111
Our Redeemer Lives	112
There Is Only One Way	113
God's Mercy	114
Unlimited Forgiveness	115
Spiritual Thoughts	116
Keep The Faith	117
Glorify God	118
He Is Coming Back	119
Jesus	120
That Great Day!	121
My Love Letter To Jesus	122
The Beginning To The End	123

"Our Creator"

"O Lord, Thou hast searched me and known me"
Psalm 139:1 (KJV)

I can hide things from you and you can hide things from me
But what we are on the inside, our Father God can see
He is omniscient, He knows us inside and out
He knows what we are capable of, with Him there is no doubt

He doesn't force His will upon us, He allows us to make a choice
But, if we listen carefully, we will hear His still, small voice
God gave us moral freedom, to choose between right and wrong
He does not force His will upon us, but
without Him we are weak, not strong
When we reject our Father's plan for us,
abuse His mercy and His grace
If not for His love and compassion, our trials alone we would face
We are born with a moral compass, which some choose to ignore
And if we do, our Father hates sin, so our ways He will deplore
Atheists deny God's existence, and Agnostics are unsure
But those of us who honor God, know He is sins only cure

"Creation"

"So God created man in His own image, in the image of
God created He him; male and female created He them. And
God blessed them and God said unto them, be fruitful and
multiply, and replenish the earth and subdue it: and have
dominion over the fish of the sea, and over the fowl of the air,
and over every living thing that moveth upon the earth."
Genesis 1:27-28 (KJV)

God created a woman from a part of a man
A woman for a man, is what God had planned
A sinless world to glorify God
A holy place where no man had trod

Then Eve beguiled by satan, tempted Adam to explore
The tree of forbidden fruit she just couldn't ignore
So, satan, God's arch enemy, from the very beginning
After Adam and Eve sinned, was sure he was winning

So God put on humanity, and became the Son of the Most High
He was willing to make the sacrifice, knowing He was going to die
He lived as a human, with no power of His own
He suffered as any man would until His Father took Him home

The End–The Beginning

"And there shall be no more curse: But the throne of God and of the Lamb shall be in it; and His servants shall serve Him."
Revelation 22:3 (KJV)

Call on Jesus, have faith that you can
He will send His Holy Spirit to help you to stand
He will be your strength, and always by your side
Til the gates of Holy Jerusalem are opened wide
And God in all His glory to us will be revealed
Before our Father, and the Lamb, we all will kneel

"God Was, Is, and Always Will be"

God created the universe; the darkness
and light became day and night
There was no one greater who could offer resistance
God spoke the Word, and the heavens came into existence

God created male and female to populate the land
They were the first of God's human creation
But their act of disobedience cause tragic devastation

They gave into temptation; ate of the tree
of knowledge of good and evil
God cast them out of Eden, and that was His reprimand
Adam and Eve journeyed far away unto another land

Women of God: Distortion and Fulfillment

She shall be called "Woman", the glory of the man
Created by God, she distorted God's plan
A woman of the bible, standing tall and full of grace
She was beguiled by satan, but still she took her place
The first mother of God's creation, to fail was her fate
She enticed the first man to sin, Adam was her mate

Many strong women did follow, not women who were questionable
But Ruth, Esther, and Mary, who were obedient, meek and humble
These women were God's chosen, they were strong in faith and love
They were highly favored, and God led them from above
Gracious, honorable, and virtuous, with God they did stand
Women of God, holy and righteous, to fulfill God's holy plan

Ruth 1:16 (KJV)

"And Ruth said, entreat me not to leave thee,
or to return from following after thee:
For whither thou goest, I will go; and where thou lodgest, I will
lodge: Thy people shall be my people, and thy God my God."

Ruth was committing herself to a life of poverty and need
But God blessed her to marry Boaz, who was very rich indeed

Jesus certainly wants us to understand and to count the cost
The Christian life is not easy, it's also about loss

We may think we are worthy, and that we deserve the best
But we will be tried like Jesus, and we will have to pass the test

"Have Faith in God"

"And Caleb stilled the people before Moses, and said, "Let us go up at once, and possess it; for we are well able to overcome it."
Numbers 13:30 (KJV)

Caleb's faith was in God
Not in the power of his own might
Because he believed and trusted in God
He was ready and willing to fight

For him there was no decision to make
Regardless of the circumstances
He was ready to step out and follow God
And with the giants, take his chances

God will fight our daily battles
And with our giants he will intercede
We don't have to be afraid
Just read His Word and take heed

"David"

"The Lord do so and much more to Jonathan: But if it
please my Father to do thee evil, then I will shew it thee,
and send thee away, that thou mayest go in peace: and the
Lord be with thee, as He hath been with my Father."
I Samuel 20:13 (KJV)

Jonathan was committed to watch over his friend
He prayed God would protect him until the end
He told David, "Don't worry, I will warn you
Watch for my sign, you'll know what to do"
Saul hated David and wanted to see him dead
David could have killed him, but walked away instead

"And it came to pass in an evening tide, that David arose
from off his bed, and walked upon the roof of the king's
house: and from the roof he saw a woman washing herself,
and the woman was very beautiful to look upon."
II Samuel 11:2 (KJV)

Sometimes we are idle, when we should be
busy and satan awakens sin in us
We convince ourselves that we are in love,
when actually, we are just in lust
Rather than accept punishment for the wrong he had done
David plotted to kill the innocent one
Uriah had no idea David had been with his wife
Or that he intended to take his life

"Solomon"

> "Give therefore thy servant an understanding heart to judge
> thy people, that I may discern between good and bad:
> for who is able to judge this thy so great a people?"
> **1st Kings 3:9 (KJV)**

Solomon prayed for wisdom and discernment to
face the challenges and struggles as King
He had no idea how to prioritize, or to take care of so many things
But, instead of asking God to remove the
challenges and struggles he would face
He was thankful that his Creator, was generous with His grace
God is a willing and joyful giver of our
daily guidance and our needs
If we repent He will forgive, and not dwell on our misdeeds

If God calls you to a task, just know that He has a plan
Trust and obey His every word, and hold on to His hand
If he has chosen you, for sure He will prepare the way
Minds and hearts will open, to receive every word you say

"Thoughts About God"

"He was in the world, and the world was made
by Him, and the world knew Him not."
John 1:10 (KJV)

God is the creator who entered His own creation;
God of heaven and earth, and God of every nation

Note: Jesus Christ is the physical manifestation of God.
Incarnation is God coming to earth as a human being

"These six things does the Lord hate: Yea, seven are an abomination
unto Him: A proud look, a lying tongue, and hands that shed
innocent blood, an heart that deviseth wicked imaginations,
feet that be swift in running to mischief, a false witness that
speaketh lies, and he that soweth discord among brethren."
Proverbs 6:16-19 (KJV)

We must keep our eyes on God, and not find fault with each other
It's discouraging to hear a saint gossip, about a sister or a brother
You may be rich or more educated, but
with God you are not exempt
There is no excuse to look down on others,
and treat them with contempt

"Behold the Lamb"

"And looking upon Jesus as He walked, he
saith, "Behold the Lamb of God!"
John 1:36 (KJV)

Behold the Lamb, the great I Am
The Passover sacrifice, that we might live
The most precious gift that God could give

The love of Jesus we share with others
And they become our sisters and brothers
Tell them Jesus says, "Come and See; take
up your cross and follow me."

"Jesus saw Nathaniel coming to Him, and saith of him,
behold an Israelite indeed, in whom is no guile!"
John 1:47 (KJV)

"Don't Judge"

Don't judge a person by where they are from,
where they live, or what they've done
Just be an example so all will see, "Jesus is real, He lives in me!"

Luke 1:30-31 (KJV)

"And the angel said unto her, fear not Mary:
for thou hast found favour with God."
"And behold, thou shalt conceive in thy womb, and
bring forth a son, and shall call His name "Jesus."

Jesus was fully human and was tempted, but without sin
If he had committed even one, our souls he could not win
He was full of compassion toward us, and
stood between God and man
He became our heavenly mediator, He became our eternal friend

"Unless thy law had been my delights, I should
then have perished in mine affliction."

Psalm 119:92 (KJV)

We need God's Word for guidance, without it we would perish
Jesus is there to remind us, as His children we are cherished
Father, we know in our hearts thy judgments are right
Help us to obey, keeping thy law is our delight

"Abomination"

"For all that do these things are an abomination unto
the Lord: and because of these abominations the Lord
thy God doth drive them out from before thee."
Deuteronomy 18:12 (KJV)

All who do these things are an abomination
God will drive out every nation
satan is darkness and Jesus is light
until the end they will continually fight
satan came to steal, kill and destroy, him we cannot trust
God sent His only Son, Jesus, who gave His life for us
Beware of those of an evil spirit; don't go where demons trod
Claim the blood of Jesus, and stay close to God

Jesus is asking, "Whom do you say that I am? Who am I to you?
Will you worship an idol god, or one you know to be true?"

Dying to self and surrendering to Jesus is
the best thing we could ever do
If we are full of ourselves and dying, there is no hope for me or you

"The Battle Is The Lord's"

"Then was Jesus led up of the Spirit into the
wilderness to be tempted of the devil."
Matthew 4:1 & 3 (KJV)

"And when the tempter came to him, he said, "If thou be the
son of God command that these stones be made bread."

In our weakest moments satan will attack
Maintain your faith, and tell him to, Get Back!
Plead the blood of Jesus, as saints we have been taught
Remind him of the battles that already have been fought
Tell him Jesus is your Saviour, the Son of the highest One
And not only did He fight him, but He has already won

"And saith unto Him, if thou be the Son of God, cast
thyself down; for it is written, he shall give His angels charge
concerning thee: and in their hands they shall bear thee
up, lest at any time thou dash thy foot against a stone."
Matthew 4:6 (KJV)

Don't allow satan to use God's Word to deceive
Read it for yourself, and then believe
We will all stand before God, and for us Jesus will plead
satan will lose the battle, he will never succeed

"Who Is To Blame?"

"Ye men of Israel, hear these words; Jesus of Nazareth, a man approved of God among you by miracles and wonders and signs, which God did by Him in the midst of you, as ye yourselves also know: Him being delivered by the determinate counsel and foreknowledge of God, ye have taken, and by wicked hands have crucified and slain:"
Acts 2:22-23 (KJV)

We killed Jesus, we all put Him on the cross
without His death, we would all be lost
But Jesus didn't remain dead, He wasn't just a martyr
He rose that we might live again and then returned to His Father

Because Jesus is Lord and Christ, alone He is able to save
This Jesus that God raised up and delivered from the grave

The crowd was filled with anguish, and
horror at what they had done
They had crucified the Messiah, God's only Son
They ran and cried to Peter, "Peter, what shall we do?"
Peter said you must repent, and then God will save you

Haggai 1:11 (KJV)

"And I called for a drought upon the land, and upon the mountains, and upon the corn, and upon the new wine, and upon the oil, and upon that which the ground bringeth for, and upon men, and upon cattle, and upon all the labour of the hands."

Everything in this world is in God's hands
So He called for a drought upon His land
Upon the mountains, the corn, and the new wine
To be restored by God in His own time

Today God can do the same
He doesn't have to feed us, or deliver us from pain
For our sins he doesn't have to forgive
But a life in hell we will surely live

"Be Humble and Upright"

"The Pharisee stood and prayed thus with himself, God, I thank thee, that I am not as other men are, extortioners, unjust, adulterers, or even as this publican."
"And the publican, standing afar off, would not lift up so much as his eyes unto heaven, but smote upon his breast, saying, God be merciful to me a sinner."

Luke 18:11-13 (KJV)

A humble spirit GOD won't ignore, but pride
and arrogance He does deplore
Glorify GOD and not yourself, for you
are no better than anyone else

"O keep my soul, and deliver me: let me not be ashamed; for I put my trust in thee."
"Let integrity and uprightness preserve me; for I wait on thee."

Psalm 25:20-21 (KJV)

Father bless me with righteousness and integrity
Glorifying you, I don't take lightly
Your requirements I strive to fulfill
With all my heart I want to do your will
You are the source of my strength, let me not be ashamed
I give you praise and honor in Jesus name

"Deliverance"

Hear my plea Lord, hear my call, You promised to be near lest I fall
Here I am on bended knee, waiting for you to deliver me

Thou art strong, but I am weak, hear me Father as I speak
Let your spirit in me be poured, and by your power be restored

"God Cares"

God cares about everything that He created, the
birds, the bees, the flowers, the trees.
Every color of every race, every person in every place
Every mountain, and every hill, everything is under His will
Every river and every ocean, there is no end to His devotion
God cares

"Lord Help Us To Stand"

"Deal bountifully with thy servant, that I
may live, and keep thy word."
Psalm 119:17 (KJV)

Lord make our roots in you like an oak tree
Let your Word abide deep inside
So the love and glory that lives in us
From the world satan cannot hide

May our hearts thirst after righteousness
Lead us Lord, please show us the way
As we strive to be our very best
In our daily walk, teach us to pray

"Pride goeth before destruction, and an haughty spirit before a fall."
Proverbs 16:18 (KJV)

Don't be proud and arrogant, don't sow what you don't want to reap
Daily read God's Holy Word, for He watches over His sheep

"Chosen People"

I Peter 2:9 (KJV)

"But you are a chosen generation, a royal priesthood, an holy nation, a peculiar people; that you should show forth the praises of Him who hath called you out of darkness into the marvelous light."

We have been called out of that miserable life of sin
And filled with the magnificent light of Jesus Christ within
As believers in Christ, we are a chosen generation
A royal priesthood; a peculiar people, and a holy nation
Our Father did more than choose us, He
gave us a story that's never been told
We were called out of darkness into the light,
and His Son Jesus saved our soul

We all belong to God, and He lives within us
When we die, and we are buried, we will go back to the dust
But when God says it's time, and Gabriel blows his horn
Hallelujah! Praise the Lord, we will all be reborn

"Comfort"

"Who comforteth us in all our tribulation, that we may be able to comfort them which are in any trouble, by the comfort wherewith we ourselves are comforted of God."
II Corinthians 1:4 (KJV)

Comfort others as God comforts you
Have compassion for what they are going through
Troubles may come, and even sorrow
We must pray for one another today and tomorrow

We should realize that there but for the grace of God, Go I
Offer love, support, and whatever it is, encourage them to try
Ask the Almighty God, please help them each day to cope
Amazing things happen when someone offers hope

We need each other on this journey
We must encourage our fellowman
And when we enter into God's Kingdom
We will walk in, hand in hand

"This Life"

"Then said Jesus unto His disciples, "If any man will come after me let him deny himself, and take up his cross, and follow Me."
Matthew 16:24 (KJV)

This life is not about you, and it's not about me
It's just our introduction to eternity
Great temptations will come, and sinners will watch us
Each and every day we must remain cautious
In the wilderness, Jesus was told by satan that He didn't have to die
Satan will approach us, but we will know what he says is a lie

We must take up our cross daily, this is what Jesus meant
Satan wants to leave God out of the picture
He thinks without Him, we will surely relent
We must see things from an eternal perspective
What we have on earth will not last
Don't focus on the days, months, or years
For soon it will all be in the past

"Satan"

"And the great dragon was cast out, that old serpent, called the
devil, and satan, which deceiveth the whole world: he was cast
out into the earth, and his angels were cast out with him."
Revelation 12:9 (KJV)

Satan is a liar and deceiver, and wants us to believe that he will win
But the Almighty God, our Saviour will be victorious in the end
Satan is our accuser both day and night,
he stands before our God but we don't have to fight
Jesus Christ is our advocate, His response was very clear,
"Get thee behind me satan," Our Lord will keep us near

Jesus will fight our battles, but we must obey and pray
Then we can look forward to seeing Him, and going home one day
Now the prince of this world shall be cast out,
satan will be defeated, there is no doubt
He is defeated by the blood of the Lamb,
Jesus's blood covers our sin, He is the great "I Am"

"A Follower of Christ"

Get thee behind me satan
I have victory over sin
King Jesus is my savior
My soul He did win

I will follow in His footsteps
As to Calvary He tread
Just as He gave His life for me
To sin I am dead

I am a follower of Christ
His light shines through me
In this world I'm His candle
For all the world to see

"Use What God Gives You"

Don't be jealous or envious
Of what God has blessed others to do
Be grateful, and thank the Lord
For what he has given to you

Whether it's speaking, singing, or praying
Just use it for God's glory
Or it may be testifying
And telling others your story

We are not here to compete with each other
God uses whomever He may choose
All of His gifts are to be desired
All of His gifts are to be used

Spiritual thought: Father, feed my spirit, feed my soul – Thank you O' God for making me whole.

"Lift Up Jesus"

"And the hand of the Lord was with them: And a great number believed, and turned unto the Lord."
Acts 11:21 (KJV)
God will not allow us to profess him in the building, and deny him in the world.

Lift up Jesus wherever you go
Let your light shine; let it glow
Don't be ashamed to mention His name
He gave his life, what a sacrifice
How can we not let the world know?
How can we not let His love show?

"Obey"

Haggai 1:5-6 (KJV)

"Now therefore thus saith the Lord of hosts; consider your ways. You have sown much, and bring in little; you eat, but you have not enough; you drink, but you are not filled with drink; you clothe you, but there is none warm; and he that earneth wages earneth wages to put it into a bag with holes."

Obeying God should be our priority
Even if it means we are the minority
You can build your mansion high on a hill
But it will not stand if not God's will
If you don't put God first, If you don't take heed
You can work all of your life and not have what you need

"Run On"

You were running well, but you kept looking back
When you focus on others you'll get off track
This is not a competition, more than one can win
The only stipulation is you must run until the end

Don't stop running and sit on the side of the road to rest
Every hour of the day you must strive to do your best
When you get weary you know God is standing by
He will lift you up and comfort you, and hold you when you cry

So, run on sisters and brothers, encourage one another and pray
Stay in the race, it won't be long, you'll be going home someday
Jesus himself will stand with you as you tell God your story
He will welcome you with open arms as you enter into glory

"Changed"

"And when He was come out of the ship, immediately there met Him out of the tombs a man with an unclean spirit,"
Mark 5:2 (KJV)

How many unclean spirits did you have before you met Christ?
Where would you be now if he hadn't changed your life?

God can fix what is broken if you obey His command
Just be still, yield, and give Him your hand

If you wish to continue in sin, you can certainly refuse
God doesn't force us, we are allowed to choose

God wants to save us, He sent His Son to intercede
If you refuse His grace and mercy, then punishment is guaranteed.

Revelation 22:3 (KJV)

"And there shall be no more curse: But the throne of God and of the Lamb shall be in it; and His servants shall serve Him."

Call on Jesus, have faith that you can
His Holy Spirit will come, and help you to stand
He will be your strength, and stand by your side
Til the gates of Holy Jerusalem, are opened wide
And God in all His glory, will be revealed
Before Him and the Lamb, we will all kneel

"Be still and know that I am God: I will be exalted among the heathen, I will be exalted in the earth."

Psalm 46:10 (KJV)

With all my heart, as long as I live
I will walk with the Lord, and be still

Romans 6:11 (KJV)

"Likewise reckon ye also yourselves to be dead indeed unto sin, alive unto God through Jesus Christ our Lord."

If you truly believe that there's nothing God can't do,
Why do you allow sin to have authority over you?
Because we are afraid to admit that we don't have to willfully sin
We constantly remind ourselves, we're not perfect, and give in

"I beseech you therefore, brethren, by the mercies of God, that ye present your bodies a living sacrifice, holy, acceptable unto God which is your reasonable service."

Romans 12:1 (KJV)

We can try to live as expected, but we will fail If not done out of love for our Saviour, and with the power of His Holy Spirit.

"More like Jesus I want to be, for my Saviour died for me"

"Every time we sin, we crucify Jesus again"

Deuteronomy 5:32 (NKJV)

"Ye shall observe to do therefore as the Lord your God hath commanded you: Ye shall not turn aside to the right hand or to the left."

Walk with the Lord, hear and obey
Hold tightly to His hand, each and every day
Remember, don't turn aside, to the left or to the right
Don't disobey God as did the Israelites

We can't always keep the law
We can try with all our might
Satan is a deceiver and a liar
And with him, we cannot fight

But, God is our protector
He is our shining light
He will always walk by our side
Morning, noon, and night

"Warranty"

Just because you are young and looking fine
Don't think your body won't decline
Or, maybe you've aged, and you're well preserved
But nothing lasts forever, or haven't you heard?

You need a warranty that only God can give
He'll take you home and that's where you'll live
Just give your heart to Jesus, and receive a life's warranty
And when you leave this old world, in heaven you will be

If you only believe, the Lord will save your soul
With your "Forever Warranty" you will never grow old
You will go with Him to your home in the sky
And live with Him forever in the sweet bye and bye

"Do Not Be Afraid"

Walk by faith, don't be overcome by fear
God Is standing by, He will always be near

God keeps His promises, remember, He cannot lie
We can stand on His Word, until the day we die

On judgment day we will see our Lord, in all of His glorious might
With sword in hand, on His white horse,
and ready for the final fight

Satan will surely be defeated, into the bottomless pit he'll be tossed
He and his demon spirits, and his followers will be lost

So don't give up, keep the faith, the King of kings will win
Walk with the Lord every day, and repent of every sin

"I Am"

"I, even I, am the Lord, and beside me there is no Saviour."
Isaiah 43:11 (KJV)

God smiles when one of His children stands up to pray
To sing a song, or to have a few words to say
He is pleased when its not, "Look at me"
But to glorify Him, as it should be
It's not a competition, just give him your best
If it's all about you, you have failed the test
We must keep our eyes on Jesus, it's all about him
Those who glorify themselves, God will condemn

"Spiritual Thoughts"

"Father take the me out of me, humble like Jesus I want to be."

"Lord in my weakness, please be my strength."

"Hold me Jesus, I need you so, be with me wherever I go."

"Here Am I Lord"

Hear my plea, Lord, hear my call
You promised to be near, lest I fall
Here am I on bended knee
Waiting for you to deliver me
Thou art strong, but I am weak
Hear me Father, as I speak
Let your spirit in me be poured
And by your power be restored

"Baby Jesus"

What can I give Him, Poor as I am?
If I were a shepherd, I could give Him a Lamb
If I were a wise man, I would never depart
What can I give Him? I can give Him my heart

Numbers 14:9 (KJV)

"Only rebel ye not against the Lord, neither fear ye the people of the land; for they are bread for us: their defense is departed from thee, and the Lord is with us: fear them not."

Sometimes we miss our blessings because
we don't have the courage to stand
Joshua and Caleb believed, and was ready to fight for the land
This is the call of the christians, we must
stand for what we believe is right
The battle is the Lord's, but we must be the light

"But my servant Caleb, because he had another spirit with him, and hath followed me fully, him will I bring into the land where into he went; and his seed shall possess it."

Numbers 14:24 (KJV)

The knowledge that God is with us, will help to build our resolve
If we are acting on God's Word, the problems will be solved
When we make a choice to live faithfully,
by what God has already said
Then we live one day at a time, and by his spirit we will be led

"Our Journey"

"But God commendeth His love toward us, in that
while we were yet sinners, CHRIST died for us."
Romans 5:8 (KJV)

We are all on a journey through life. None of us are perfect so
we should not be judgmental or, HOLIER THAN THOU.
God knows where we fall short, and He is merciful and
forgiving. You can't encourage others to reach the point where
you are in your Christian journey if you are not willing to
share, and admit to the struggle you had getting there.

"Let everything that hath breath praise
the Lord, Praise ye the Lord."

Psalm 150:6 (KJV)

O Lord you are worthy of our praise morning, noon, and night
Before lying down, and when we rise at morning light
Let your honor and your glory be seen in all that we do
Almighty God, our creator, to show our love for you

Philippians 2:3 (KJV)

"Let nothing be done through strife and vain glory, but in lowliness of mind let each esteem other better than themselves."

"Not Your Glory"

Don't use your gifts to glorify yourself
It's not just about you, but everyone else
God has given us all gifts, to draw others to His light
But no one will be blessed, if we squabble and fight
Let others see the love, the joy, the peace and unity
That although we may stumble, our Lord has set us free
We are one body in Christ, our aim is just to glorify Him
If we cause someone to turn away, our lights will be eternally dim.

"The Power of Love"

The power of Jesus's love for us put Him on the cross
The power of God's love for Jesus brought Him from the grave
The Power of our love for Jesus, should make us want to be saved

Lord Save Us!

Save us Jesus, never leave us alone
Let us stand in peace before your throne

As brothers and sisters let us be known
Hand in hand we will follow you home

As we pray for one another please hear our plea
The sick, the wounded, and the hungry

We lift up to you those filled with hate
Save them Lord, before it's too late

Father fill us with the fruit of your spirit; love, faith, peace, joy, gentleness, goodness, meekness, long suffering, and self control…….in Jesus name

"Beauty in The Desert"

There is beauty in the dust
There is beauty in all of us
Everything was created by God's hand
So there is beauty all over the land
There is beauty in the green grass
There is beauty in the ocean so blue
There is beauty in the mountains so high
There is beauty in the cloud covered sky
There is beauty in everything that God created
And no matter what we may presume
Beauty is in the desert, where the prickly cactus bloom

"Wrinkles"

We all have some wrinkles
And the iron is God's Word
You may think little sins are crinkles
But that's not what I've heard

Sin is sin sisters and brothers
So we have to turn up the heat
A warm iron won't be sufficient
If the Saviour we plan to meet

If we spray a little starch
Maybe the wrinkles won't return
Get them all out now
Or with satan we will burn

Jesus is our intercessor
And He won't leave a crease
So when we leave this old world
We'll all have heavenly peace

Thanksgiving and Praise

Thank you Father for your love, grace and mercy
Thank you for your gift of prayer
Thank you Father for all your many blessings
Thank you for always being there

Remember Jesus on the cross
He gave His life so we wouldn't be lost
Lord let your glory be revealed
Let the world see that God is real

Lord at your feet I humbly kneel
By your power let me be filled
Lord all that I am and all that I'll ever be
I humbly yield myself to thee

God will provide all we need to live for Christ
He won't feed our greed with riches, but a God filled contented life

"If God Is Not In You, He Is Not In The Building"

"I wonder why so many people keep going from church to church?" One of the sisters asked. The response was, "they are church hoppers." They don't want to be here anyway, so they look for things to discourage themselves. They look for excuses not to be here.

Then one of the church mothers said, "We can keep making excuses for our behavior. All these people are not "Church Hoppers". They don't all like going from church to church. We need to examine ourselves and accept some of the responsibility for what the problem is, and some of it is us. If people are hearing us saying one thing and seeing us doing another, we are, "Stumbling Blocks," and God is not pleased. Our godliness should be a reflection of Jesus Christ. If we only pray when we are in church, if we only read God's Word when we are in church, if we only show love for one another when we are in church, they may be, "Church Hoppers", but we are "Stumbling Blocks". If God is not in us, then God is not in this building.

Haggai 1:13 (KJV)

"Then spoke Haggai the Lord's messenger unto the people, saying, I am with you, saith the Lord."

God promises to provide
Our needs to fulfill
He said, "I am with you",
And He is with us still

"Then saith the damsel that kept the door unto Peter, art not thou also one of this man's disciples? He saith, I am not."
John 18:17 (KJV)

When we are high in the spirit, we think
we could never deny Christ
And yet when we should speak up for
what's right, we fear for our life

Simon Peter said he would never deny
Jesus; that He would rather die
and yet, when he was questioned, He told lie, after lie, after lie

"One Prayer at A Time"

When I'm cold, you keep me warm, when I'm tired you give me rest
When I'm hungry you feed me, you always help me to be my best

One prayer at a time

When I'm lonely, you hold me, when I'm sick you ease my pain
When I'm weak, you are my strength,
you're the one who keeps me sane

One Prayer at a Time

When I'm lost, you find me, you lead me back where I belong
You lead me back where I should be, you're
always there to keep me strong

One Prayer at a Time

"In Your Own Time"

Father, Im not going to ask you to stop this storm
I know that you know what is best
But I will ask that you strengthen us, Lord
And help us to pass the test

We know that everything happens for a reason
Even though we don't understand
The earth is the LORD's and the fulness thereof
And we are all in your hand
There are those who think they are in control,
Their money is their power,
But, Lord, I know you are coming back,
Though I don't know the minute or the hour

"God's Grace"

Trust in his power, pray for God's grace
Prepare to stand before him, to see him face to face
We are all going to struggle, against the corruption of sin
Without the holy spirit, it's impossible to win
Jesus is the victor, the Saviour of our soul
Hallelujah, glory to god, his blood has made us whole

"Honor thy father and mother; I which is the
first commandment with promise;"
Ephesians 6:2 (KJV)

As we seek to live out our identity in Christ,
It's not enough being a good husband or wife.
Our children watch everything that we do,
So, our love for Christ must always show through.

"Faith"

"Now faith is the substance of things hoped for, the evidence of things not seen." Hebrews 11:1 (KJV)

> Step out on faith: encourage others when you do
> We glorify our Saviour with the trials that we go through
> Let others see your walk with the Lord:
> Let them see he has the world in his hand
> When trials come and times are hard
> Only God can help us to stand
> Only God has the authority to bless
> He strengthens us with joy and hope
> Only Jesus, by the grace of God
> Can give us the strength to cope

"Beloved, believe not every spirit, but try the spirits whether they are of God: Because many false prophets are gone out into the world." I John 4:1 (KJV)

> Don't be deceived, God is not dead
> You just can't believe everything that is said
> Try the spirit by the spirit
> Meditate on God's Word
> Then you will know that it's true
> And not just what was heard

"Steppin High"

"But he that glorieth, let him glory in the Lord, for not he that commendeth himself is approved, but whom the Lord commendeth."
  ll Corinthians 10:17-18

So, you're steppin high with a smile on your face
You had people shouting all over the place
"Girl, you sang that song", and your smile got wide
Yes, you were obviously filled with pride
Then God shook you, and said, "Did you forget about me?
    Without my power, where would you be?
You said, "O Lord, Im sorry, I didn't give you the praise instead,
    I let all this adoration go to my head.
    Please, forgive me, Lord hear my plea,
It will never happen again, just you wait and see."

"I Never Got the Church in Me"

Lord, I was raised in the church. I went to Sunday school, Y.P.W.W., B.Y.P.U, Bible Study, and Prayer Meeting. I never missed church. I joined church when I was young, and I was faithful. I sang in the choir, served on the usher board, and was involved in all the committees: I worked hard in the church. Now, I'll admit I lied sometimes, slandered other people's names, and spread a lot of gossip, caused a lot of hate, misunderstandings, and confusion, but I never missed church. I cheated and stole things that didn't belong to me, (a little money when the deacons weren't looking.) I even kept quiet when someone else was blamed for what I did, but I never missed church. I stayed angry with some of my family members and friends because I refused to say I was sorry. Why should I apologize? I wouldn't sit or stand next to people of other races, or even talk to them. Lord, I know it's a sin to hate, so I didn't hate them, I just didn't like them. Well, I did hate white people because of what they did to the Indians and the black people; and I know those people were long dead, and I know even then there were some good white folks. I hated the Jews because of what they did to you, Lord. I know they all weren't responsible, but still. Oh, I know you are a Jew, and I love you Lord, that's why I never missed church. I may have fornicated, committed adultery, engaged in a few unnatural relationships, but Lord, I never missed church!

What? Go straight to hell? But Lord, I never missed church. I was there every time the doors opened. Oh, I see……I never got the church in me. Is that what you said, Lord? I NEVER GOT THE CHURCH IN ME.

"My Intercessor"

"In the same way, the Spirit helps us in our weakness, we do not know what we ought to pray for, but the Spirit Himself intercedes for us through wordless groans,"
Romans 8:26 (KJV)

It's good to know my prayers are heard
That God is listening to every word
For everything that my heart does yearn
I know that it's my Father's concern
He listens to my every moanMy prayers are daily before His throne

"Spiritual Thoughts"

"Lord, if I stumble, If I fall, I know you will always hear my call"
"Yes to your will, yes to your way, in the name of Jesus, Lord I pray"
"Pray, pray, pray, close to God we must stay"

"God Is Using You"

Two are better than one, this race we have got to run
When someone is sick and God leads you to pray
Or maybe when they stumble and fall by the way
Or, perhaps they are just tired, and all worn out
And you lift them up in prayer, there is no doubt-----
God is using you

When someone is discouraged and think they can't succeed
And within your heart, to God for them you plead
When your heart is aching, and they are feeling weak
God listens, and He leads you to speak.......
God is using you

"Light in the Lord"

"For ye were sometimes darkness, but now are ye light in the Lord: walk as children of light;"
Ephesians 5:8 (KJV)

Let your light reflect the holiness of God
Light up the darkness like a lightning rod
Jesus said, "We are the light of the world"
So let's be an example for every boy and girl
Don't be afraid to be different, we are not children of the night
We are followers of Jesus, the children of the light
Let the light of Jesus shine and pray that it doesn't grow dim
For every time we choose the world, we stop glorying Him

"Be Prepared"

"For as the lightning cometh out of the east, and shineth even unto the west: So shall also the coming of the Son of man be."
Matthew 24:27 (KJV)

To prepare for Christ's return, into His work we must invest
Within the church, and outside of it, we must give our very best
He said the sun shall fall from heaven, oh
my, what an awesome sight!
Then our Saviour will appear after the trumpet sound,
And Glory Hallelujah! We'll all be heaven bound!

"Stay in The Race"

> "Wherefore seeing we also are compassed about with so great a cloud of witnesses, let us lay aside every weight, and the sin which doth so easily beset us, and let us run with patience the race that is set before us."
> **Hebrews 12:1 (KJV)**

Despite our trials and persecution
We must remain focused on God
Remember the ones gone on before us
For we are traveling the path they trod

God loves all of his children
But will chastise and rebuke us for sin
We must not give up or become discouraged
He will be with us until the end

So lift up your hands and praise Him
And make straight paths with your feet
Be an example for your sisters and brothers
And one day in heaven we'll meet

"First Encounter"

"And He said unto them, these are the words
which I spoke unto you, while I was
yet with you, that all things must be fulfilled,
which were written in the law of
Moses, and in the prophets, and in the Psalms,
concerning me, then opened He
their understanding, that they might understand the scriptures."
Luke 24:44-45 (KJV)

When was you first encounter with Jesus?
From the beginning was it made clear?
Were you filled with joy or sorrow,
Or like the disciples, filled with fear?

Jesus said, look for Him in the scriptures
Through my words, your faith will increase
Seek and ye shall find
And your doubts and fears will cease

Following Christ means striving to do the same things He would do
When you struggle, just remember, He gave His life for you

"Pressing On"

God loves me and I love me, so here is how it's going to be
You can talk about me, you can tear me down
But with God I stand on holy ground
I'm Pressing On

Covered by the blood of Christ, I'll serve the Lord the rest of my life
I may cry, but I will not fear
For my Father is always near
I'm Pressing On

I will press toward the mark……..
Here am I Lord, here am I
Use me, use me
Until I die

"God's Candles"

> "Let your light so shine before men, that they may see our good works, and glorify your Father which is in heaven."
> **Matthew 5:16 (KJV)**

As followers of Christ, His light shines
through us for all the world to see
We who are saved are His candles, He uses you and me
Choosing to take the fate we deserved, Jesus died in our place
He never sinned, but chose a death He didn't have to face
He has the key to hell and death, He is the first and the last
When He says, "I know you not", into hell you will be cast
Jesus has won the battle, His Word has made this clear
Satan is already defeated, and we have nothing to fear
One day it will all be over, our transformation will be complete
Jesus will proclaim, "Not Guilty", when we kneel at our Father's feet

"He Lives"

The power of God gives us the strength to endure
The love of Christ will keep us secure
Satan is evil and will try to condemn
But God said nothing will separate us from Him
He Lives
In the garden of Gethsamane
My Lord Jesus prayed for me
I thank God for my life
And for His Son Jesus Christ
He Lives
Why seek the living among the dead
Jesus has risen just as He said
He defeated death just for us
We can live again through faith and trust
He lives
Jesus said, "Only believe, handle me and see,"
I am the living Saviour who died on Calvary
He lives
Remember Jesus died on the cross
He gave His life so we wouldn't be lost
He lives

"Three in One"

"And Jesus, when He was baptized, went up straightway out of the water: and lo, the heavens were opened unto Him, and He saw the Spirit of God descending like a dove, and lighting upon Him: and lo a voice from heaven, saying, this is my Beloved Son, in whom I am well pleased."
Matthew 3:16-17 (KJV)

The Holy Trinity: The Father, The Son, and The Holy Spirit, all present at the same time.

"Doubt"

John Doubted (Matthew 11:2-6) (KJV)

The Disciples Doubted (Matthew 28:16-17) (KJV)

We have all certainly had our moments of doubt; satan is on his job, but God is real and one day He will return.

God is patient with us, He gives us many chances, over and over again to turn away from sin, to believe in Him. His patience does not mean that we should procrastinate, that it will never be too late, or that we will always get another chance. His patience will not last forever.

The bible gives us insight into who God is: God is love, God is forgiving, God is patient, God is all knowing, God is jealous, God is all powerful-----God is coming again!

"We Can't Hide"

"O Lord, thou hast searched me, and known me."
Psalm 139:1 (KJV)

I can hide things from you and you can hide things from me;
But what we truly are, our Father God can see
He is omniscient, He knows us inside out
He knows what we are capable of
With Him there is no doubt
He doesn't force His will upon us, He allows us to make a choice
But, if we listen carefully, we will hear His still small voice

"I will praise thee, for I am fearfully and wonderfully made."

Psalm 139:14 (KJV)

God knows me better than I know myself,
He created me and everyone else
Male and female, we came from the dust
Created by God, who is holy and just

"A Holy Life"

There will be challenges and struggles that we all must face
Instead of asking God to move them, we should ask for His grace

For through them all He will be with us,
He will always be our guide
He will never leave us or forsake us, He will remain by our side

Pray for wisdom and discernment, and obey not what you heard
But work daily for your Master, and read His Holy Word

"He hath made every thing beautiful in His time:
also He hath set the world in their heart,
So that no man can find out the work that God
maketh from the beginning to the end."
Ecclesiastes 3:11 (KJV)

Father, this deep longing only you can fill
Our hearts and our souls to you we yield
An instinct for you Lord has been implanted in us
Deep down inside, we know who to trust
O' God our Father, you are our hearts true home
We shall return to you, no matter how far we roam

"Submission"

"Wives submit yourselves unto your own
husband, as unto the Lord."
Ephesians 5:22 (KJV)

A man who loves the Lord, a good wife he will find
The best that God has to offer, a woman who is loving and kind
Husbands love your wives, no matter what you must go through
This woman that God has blessed you to have, is not a part of you

Jesus said, "Lo, I am with you always", so He
will be there through the good times and
the bad, the joyful and the sad……..

"And why beholdest thou the mote that is in thy
brother's eye, but considerest not the
beam that is in thine own eye?"
Matthew 7:3 (KJV)

Just A Thought:
Don't point your finger to reprove another
Take a look at yourself, not your sister and brother

"In God's Service"

You may sing in the choir, you may pray in a pew
You may preach in the pulpit, but if God is not in you…
It's all in vain
You may be on the Mother's Board, or an usher at the door
You may be a Deacon… need I say more?
But if God is not in you It's all in vain

To know the Lord fills you with joy and praise
If you love the Lord, you will walk in His ways

Just A Thought:
"To diligently keep thy precepts, Lord
On our own we cannot do

We need the power of our Holy Spirit
As we daily walk with you" move up!

Just A Thought

Father, yes to your will, yes to your way,
lead us and guide us every day.

Philippians 3:18-19 (KJV)

"For many walk, of whom I have told you
often, and now tell you even weeping,
That they are the enemies of the cross of Christ:
whose end is destruction, whose
God is their belly, and whose glory is in their
shame, who mind earthly things."

Many walk, but only a few follow Christ
Study the Word for yourself
Remember, this is your life

"And they brought him unto Him: And when he saw Him, straightway the spirit tare him; and he fell on the ground and wallowed foaming."

Mark 9:20 (KJV)

Demon spirits may be all around
They may cast you screaming to the ground
By God's power you'll be able to withstand
They must obey God's holy command
No matter how bad the devastation
God can change the situation

"Press Toward the Mark"

"I PRESS TOWARD THE MARK FOR THE PRIZE OF THE HIGH CALLING OF GOD IN CHRIST JESUS."
Philippians 3:14 (KJV)

If Jesus, who was God, was humble as our Saviour
We should all honour him and imitate his behavior
He came down from glory, humble all the way to the cross
Without his loving sacrifice, our souls would be lost
We all have a race to run, we strive to pass the test
We know our God is forgiving, yet he wants our very best
We don't have to walk blindly, God's arms are open wide
He will always walk beside us, he is our daily guide

Just A Thought:
We must press toward the mark, the prize cannot be bought
For Jesus didn't give up, when satan for us he fought

"If"

If you were black and I was white, how would
you feel if I didn't treat you right?
If I thought you weren't important and I looked down on you,
no matter how educated, intelligent, or what you could do?
You can treat others any way you want, do anything you
please; shoot us and beat us, and hang us from trees
You have no fear of reprimand because of who you are,
But, there is a God who will make you pay
Because, you have gone too far!

"Lord We Need You So"

Weaknesses, doubts, fears, anxieties, sickness,
disease, death, low self-esteem,
Loneliness, stress, idiosyncrasies, desires,
needs, wants, trials, temptations…..
LORD WE NEED YOU SO.

when trouble comes and I get discouraged, Lord I trust you still
But, my heart gets heavy when I'm kind
of low; I can't help how I feel
I just need you to hold me Jesus, just whisper in my ear
When I feel your love, and hear your voice,
I'll know that you are near
I'll know that everything will be alright, my Father is in control
The battle belongs to Him, and He is strong and bold

"Blessed are they that keep His testimonies and
that seek Him with the whole heart."

Psalm 119:2 (KJV)

God promised us blessings if we walk in His way
If we keep His testimonies, read His Word and pray

"Vain Glory"

Philippians 2:3 (KJV)
"Let nothing be done through strife or vain glory; but in lowliness of mind let each esteem other better than themselves."
Don't use your gifts to glorify yourself
It's not just about you, but everyone else
God has given us all gifts to draw others to His light
But no one will be blessed if we squabble and fight
Let others see the love, the joy, the unity
That although we may stumble, our God has set us free

"God's Love"

The power of Jesus' love for us put Him on the cross
The power of God's love for Jesus brought Him from the grave
The power of our love for Jesus should make us want to be saved

"A Friend"

ll Corinthians 5:11 (KING JAMES VERSION)

"Knowing therefore the terror (A reverential awe of God in light of His perfect holiness, righteousness, omniscience, and omnipotence, that leads a person to live in obedience to Him.) of the Lord, we persuade men; but we are made manifest unto God; and I trust also are made manifest in our consciences."

With deep love and respect we are motivated to spread the news
Knowing the terror of the Lord, men are persuaded to choose

With reverential awe for an amazing God in all His holiness
As we stand before Him, as our judge,
we'll know we've done our best
"Therefore if any man be in Christ, he is a new creature: old things are passed away; behold, all things are become new."
II Corinthians 5:17 (KJV)

A friend in Christ is a true friend, they will
stick by you through thick and thin
You can love them freely and they won't abuse you,
you can be yourself and they won't misuse you
During the hard times they won't depart, a
friend in Christ loves from the heart

Revelation 1:18 KJV

"I am He that liveth, and was dead, and, behold, I am alive for evermore, Amen; and have the keys of hell and of death."

"It's Over"

Choosing to take the penalty we deserved, Jesus died in our place
He never sinned, but chose a death that he didn't have to face

He has the keys to hell and death, He is the first and the last
When he says, "I know you not," into hell you will be cast

Jesus has won the battle, His Word has made this clear
Satan is already defeated, and we have nothing to fear

One day it will all be over, our transformation will be complete
Jesus will proclaim, "Not Guilty", when we kneel at our Father's feet

No one can say they don't know God for he
is revealed through His creation
There is no excuse for not believing in Him, when the
day comes for God to judge, there will be no excuse.

"Forgiveness"

In grief and despair the Lord I sought
He heard my cry, and with satan He fought
Oh Lord God, I sinned, I confess
Forgive me, please, for I cannot rest
My heart is heavy, I have fallen from grace
I tremble in fear to see your face
But as I stood before Him, filled desperately with need
From the depth of my soul, with my savior I did plead
Then the, "Joy of the Lord", filled my soul
He said, "I forgive you", and I was made whole

"Blackness"

Blackness: Not the color of one's skin, but
what emanates from deep within
That hatred toward our fellowman is not a part of God's own plan
Blackness: It's a sickness that destroys the soul,
and only God can make us whole
It runs so deep within your mind, you want to
kill, and destroy, whoever you can find
Blackness: We've passed it on from generation to
generation; it's destroying our families and our nation
It's in our schools, our homes, our government,
it's past time for us to repent
Blackness: Will we ever just look at each other
and see another sister or brother?
Not because they look the same, but realize they are not to blame.
Blackness: Satan is running rampant, but God has shown
us favor, He sent His only Son to change our behavior.

To tear down the walls of hatred, bigotry, jealousy, envy, and strife
To penetrate the blackness, to dispel darkness and bring new life.
All the blackness will be shattered as we watch God's plan unfurl
We'll see the Holy City Jerusalem descend into God's new world

"God Wants Us All To Be Winners"

It's God's intention that the gospel spread all over His creation
That His church be made up of people of
every tribe, tongue, and nation
We are all the same in God's eyes
Created He him every shape and size
Flowers and trees no one can supersede
Everything on this earth came from God's seed
Spiritual growth is a lifelong process
God speaks to our hearts and gives us access
Encouragement must be repeated over and over again
Jesus is our mediator, Jesus is our friend
We must love the Lord with all our heart
Seek His ways and never depart
God loves us, but admits He's jealous
To please Him we must be zealous
If we love Him and obey His command
We'll walk into heaven hand in hand

"Disciples"

"And they continued stedfastly in the apostles doctrine and fellowship, and in breaking of bread, and in prayers."
Acts 2:42 (KJV)

You pray for me, I'll pray for you
Let the world see Jesus in all that we do
Let us worship and praise together
And share a loving meal
A family of God of every race
Genuine and real

"And sold their possessions and goods, and parted them to all men, as every man had need."
Acts 2:45

God gives us caring spirits, and gives us enough to share
If you hoard all that you have for yourself
You are definitely in need of prayer

Jesus is the answer; this message we must get across
He said, pray, care and share
To disobey is our loss

Matthew 8:5-6 (KJV)

"And when Jesus was entered into Capernaum,
there came unto Him a Centurian,
Beseeching Him and saying, Lord, my servant lieth at
home sick of the palsy, grievously tormented."

Roman or Jew, Black or White
Jesus came to shine His light
His gospel wasn't limited to one people or one nation
God sent His only Son for all His creation

Jesus told a desperate world, "I'll bring hope and healing with me"
And all the lost souls looked to Him, and
said, "Lord I trust in thee."
Jesus had authority, when He spoke He was heard
He had all power in His hand, all He did was speak the Word

Psalm 119:23 (KJV)

"Princes also did sit and speak against me: But
thy servant did meditate in thy statutes."

No matter what others may say or do
Focus on God, and he will lead you
Your strength and joy is in His Word
Let His spirit lead you, for some have not heard

You must remember to live it, and to teach
Then others you will surely reach
Be humble, not full of pride
Your weaknesses, don't try to hide
Then one day you will realize your fate
And walk with the Lord through the pearly gate

"I'm Up High, Now I Can Breathe"

Lord, I passed through the storms, I walked through the rain
I suffered through a lot of sickness, I struggled with a lot of pain
With all of my trials, and troubles too, I never would have made it
If not for you
You told me to come up high, and now I can breathe
You said, "Take my hand, you don't have to leave
I know it was hard, but you gave your best,
Now you can breathe, so sit and rest."
I'm up high, now I can breathe……..

JUST A THOUGHT:
Don't worry, God is never blind to your tears, never deaf to your prayers, and never uncaring about your pain…..
He sees all, knows all, hears all; and He cares

I Corinthians 13:1-3 (KJV)

"Though I speak with the tongues of men and of angels, and have not love, I am become as sounding brass, or a tinkling cymbol. And though I have the gift of prophecy, and understand all mysteries, and all knowledge; and though I have all faith, so that I could remove mountains, and have not love, I am nothing. And though I bestow all my goods to feed the poor, and though I give my body to be burned, and have not love, it profiteth me nothing."

Bigots

There are bigots everywhere and in every race; bigots who claim they love the Lord, and that's certainly a disgrace

Bigots in organizations, supposedly for all peoples, in schools, and government, and some churches with the highest steeples

You may be able to fool your family, and even your closest friends, but the one who really knows your heart, will hold you accountable at the end

"Peace In The Midst of A Storm"

We often face spiritual and emotional
storms; terrifying circumstances
We must keep the faith, trust in the Lord,
pray, and take our chances
And God will give us peace in the midst of our storm………..

"I Am Your Vessel"

I just need you to hold me Jesus: Teach me, lead me, guide me, heal me, fix me, cleanse me, prepare me, feed me, melt me, mold me, make me, break me, shape me; Do with me as you will.

Hold me Jesus, hold me; melt me and mold me
Grace and peace you've shown me
Completeness and wholeness in my life
The effect of God's work through Jesus Christ
If I fall, if I stumble, lift me up Lord, and
keep me humble: I am you vessel

"Be still and know that I am God: I will be exalted among the heathen, I will be exalted in the earth."
Psalm 46:10 (KJV)

With all my heart, as long as l live
I will walk with the Lord, and be still

Psalm 119:92-93 (KJV)

"Unless thy law had been my delights, I should then
have perished in my affliction. I will never forget thy
precepts: For with them thou hast quickened me."

Jesus, who was fully human was tempted, but without sin
If He had committed even one, our souls He could not win
He was full of compassion toward us, and
stood between God and men
He became our mediator, He became our eternal friend

We need God's holy word for guidance, without it we would perish
Jesus is there to remind us, as His children we are cherished
Father, we know in our hearts that your judgments are right
Help us obey you, and let your laws be our delight

Spiritual Thoughts

God is faithful, God is just, God is worthy of our trust
To our prayers we get God's response; He will answer
Faith does not need material evidence

"He Will Never Leave Us or Forsake Us"

When we are tired, when we are weary
Jesus will be near whatever betide
When like lost sheep, we tend to stray,
He will always be our guide

If we willfully sin or disobey
We can expect a reprimand
But He will always be standing by
With a loving outstretched hand

We may have to struggle
It may take months or years
But He will always be there
To dry all our tears

So, hold on, don't become discouraged
Don't let go of God's unchanging hand
Rest in peace and one day soon, You'll
wake up in the promised land

"Hear and Obey"

"And Moses said unto God, who am I, that I
should go unto Pharoah, and that I should bring
forth the children of Israel out of Egypt?"
Exodus 3:11 (KJV)

Fear not, neither be dismayed, your God will go before thee
Just walk with him in faithfulness, love and humility
Who God calls, He will prepare
You are His vessel, so be aware
He will endow you with power, to face what you must
Just step out on faith, and a little trust
Signs and wonders God will perform
You will see His power in the midst of your storm
Open your mouth and don't be afraid
God will speak through you, your mouth He made
Don't dwell on self-perception, you are in God's hands
You are His chosen vessel, just obey as He commands

"Be A Faithful Witness"

"And ye are witnesses of these things"
Luke 24: 48

God is in the Old Testament
And He is the same God in the new
Whichever one you choose to read
You'll be judged by the wrong you do
A God of love, forgiveness and grace
The one true God we all must face

When you profess to be a Christian
People are watching you
Deep down they may want to believe
So be careful of what you do
If you cause one of God's children to stumble
Or to turn away from Him
The blood of Jesus won't cover you
And you will be condemned

"Sin"

"As it is written, there is none righteous, no not one."
Romans 3:10 (KJV)

We have Adam to thank for our sinful
nature, evil runs rampant among us
The list goes on and on, as we lie, disobey and lust

If you think you will never sin, you are
fighting a battle you can't win
No matter how righteous you may be, without Jesus you are guilty

"Power"

> "He giveth power to the faint; and to them that
> have no might he increaseth strength."
> **Isaiah 40:29 (KJV)**

Lord by your stripes we are healed, with your power we are filled
You giveth strength to the meek, and increase the power of the weak

"The Whole Armour of God"

"Put on the whole armour of God, that you may be
able to stand against the wiles of the devil."
Ephesians 6:11 (KJV)

Stay in God's Word and He'll be there even when you are weak
When satan starts to attack, to your spirit He will speak
Put all your hope in God's strength and the power of His might
Satan is our adversary, but this is not our fight……..
The battle is the Lords

"Stand"

"Stand therefore, having your loins girt about with truth,
and having on the breastplate of righteousness."
Ephesians 6:14 (KJV)

We must stand firm in who we are in Christ
Remember, our Saviour gave his life
The whole armour of God is guaranteed
Obey God's Word, it's all that we need
The belt, the breastplate, and the boots
We must dig deep to strengthen our roots
The shield, the helmet, and the sword
The power of God, our heavenly Lord

"Our Redeemer Lives"

"But now thus saith the Lord that created thee, O Jacob, and He that formed thee, O Israel, fear not: For I have redeemed thee, I have called thee by thy name; Thou art mine."
Isaiah 43:1 (KJV)

God redeemed us in the past
With a love that will forever last
He said in His Word, "Thou art mine"
And He will protect us til the end of time

Sometimes he will allow us to suffer
For the choices that we make
But, He is always there to help us
When it's more than we can take

God loves us so much
He will pay any ransom or cost
He sent His only Son Jesus
Who died on the cross

He promised us prosperity
But not always materialistic
So, when we pray and ask for things
We must be realistic

"There Is Only One Way"

"Jesus saith unto him, I am the way, the truth, and the life: No man cometh unto the Father but my me."
John 14:6 (KJV)

Jesus is the way, we must listen to His voice
Hear and obey, He gives us a choice
Jesus is the way, to the world He is the light
We must walk in His footsteps, not struggle and fight
We know in our hearts, He is the only way
And from His side we must not stray
Satan is busy walking to and fro
But to our Father we can always go
His Holy Spirit is our guide every day
We must read His word, obey and pray

"God's Mercy"

> "Let thy mercies come also unto me, O Lord,
> even thy salvation, according to thy word."
> **Psalm 119:41 (KJV)**

The mercies of our Lord is unchanging and unending
Always unconditional when our hearts need mending
Don't hesitate to pray to God for deliverance from distress
Our trials and tribulations are only a test
God sent His only Son that through Him we might be saved
He endured pain and heartache and by Judas, He was betrayed
Because of God's love, grace, and mercy we are forgiven of our sin
Because of Jesus, heavens wonder, satan cannot win

"Unlimited Forgiveness"

"He saith unto him the third time, Simon, son of Jonah, lovest thou me? Peter was grieved because He said unto him the third time, lovest thou me? And he said unto Him, "Lord thou knowest all things; thou knowest that I love thee." Jesus saith unto him, "Feed my sheep."
John 21:17 (KJV)

After we have sinned we may feel hopelessly lost
But by the renewing mercies of God, Jesus paid the cost
Past sins, hurts and failures, whatever is our story
God forgives, God restores, He uses us for His glory
He will forgive us no matter what we have done
The battle is not over til the final race is run
The relationship will be restored to all that it's worth
No greater love is found anywhere on this earth
Our slate will be wiped clean, and we'll be homeward bound
We'll climb the stairway to heaven and receive our golden crown

"Spiritual Thoughts"

Lord, I'm not all that I should be, but all that I am, I yield to thee.

Help me Father to hear and obey, and not be
concerned about what others may say.

God is always there for me and you, there is
nothing too hard for Him to do.

Help me Father, help me please, while I kneel on bended knees.

More like Jesus I want to be, for my Saviour died for me.

Help me Father to bear fruit, to leave an impact on others
To mentor and influence, be an example for my sisters and brothers.

Yes to your will, yes to your way
Lord I want to please you every day

Believe me, there is a God, beware of what you do
You are a part of His creation, and He is watching you

Passing through troubled waters filled with pain and sorrow
Calling on the "Almighty God," our only hope for tomorrow

"Keep The Faith"

When we ask something of God, and He doesn't answer right away
We must keep the faith and continue to pray

We must rely on God in spite of our fear
For even when we doubt, God is always near

Waiting on God is not a waste of time
So continue to pray, stay attached to the vine

If someone stands against you, and you
sincerely believe you are right
Just be still, and do God's will, this is not your fight

Keep The Faith

"Glorify God"

"Even everyone that is called by my name: For I have created him for my glory, I have formed him; yea I have made him."
Isaiah 43:7 (KJV)

Glorify God in all that you do
Afterall He created you
You are not your own
You belong to the Father
Instead of forgiving
He could make life harder

Get thee behind me satan
For I have victory over sin
King Jesus is my Saviour
My soul He did win
I will follow in His footsteps
As to calvary He tread
He gave His life for all of us
To sin I am dead
As I daily walk in His word
In my heart He will abide
And when I enter the portals of glory
The doors will open wide

"He Is Coming Back"

You may fool the people, you can scream, jump and shout
But God looks on the heart, so for Him there will be no doubt
If you're a liar, or a deceiver, or if you're just full of hate
You won't be allowed to enter in, you'll be left outside the gate

THOUGHTS:
Believe in Jesus, one day He will return, but
without faith you will surely burn.

Here I am Lord, hear am I, help me to hold on until I die.

Read His word, believe and obey, shout
and rejoice, He's coming anyday!

Jesus

Oh to have been there, my Saviour I would have sought
To see Him standing on the mountain, to listen as He taught

To feel His love and compassion as He touched those in distress
To witness the blind seeing, the lame
walking, so many people blessed

To see thousands gathered together, just to watch His every motion
To sit for hours and hours, to show such utter devotion

To share the three little fishes and the five loaves of bread
To be one of the five thousand hungry people that were fed

I would like to have seen Peter step out of
the boat before he could think
When he lost his faith and cried, "Lord save
me", and suddenly started to sink

Oh, and I must not forget His friend Lazarus,
whom He awakened from sleep
He showed Mary and Martha they had no cause to weep

I wasn't there as a witness, but I'm saved by His grace
Sometimes I stumble, sometimes I fall, but I'm staying in the race

"That Great Day!"

When God calls Jesus, and says, "It's Time"
Will you be saved, or still running blind
That great day will be a day of trouble and distress
A day of darkness, waste, and gloominess
That great day God's trumpet will sound
No need to try to hide for you will be found
Neither your silver nor your gold will save you that day
When God says it's time Jesus will be on His way
We will kneel at God's feet and Jesus will proclaim
Either heaven or hell, and call you by name
The pearly gates will open wide
And some with Jesus as He steps inside
Those who are washed in the Blood of the Lamb
Will live forever after with the great "I AM"

"My Love Letter To Jesus"

Dear Jesus,
I love you, and thank you for loving me
I thank you for the sacrifice that you made way back on Calvary
I thank you for your holy word, the messages that you left behind
And I love to read about the thousands you fed,
and how you gave sight to the blind

You walked and talked with your disciples, and
taught them to have faith and to obey
You told them about God, the Father, and that you are the only way
Oh, and how you brought your friend Lazarus back from the dead
He heard his Lord and Saviour calling and from the tomb he tread

You left your peace and Holy Spirit and joined your Father on high
But the day will soon come, I truly believe,
when I will see your face in the sky

"The Beginning To The End"

Our country is a racially divided nation
It started at the beginning of creation
Families and friends turned against each other
Satan is busy setting brother against brother

God sent His Son a long time ago
But by His people He was condemned
Because of their pride and arrogance
They just refused to receive Him

Now one day He will come in all His glory
Surrounded by His heavenly host
The gospels tell all of the story
Of the Father, Son, and the Holy Ghost